AN EXPLORATION
OF CONSCIENCE

AN EXPLORATION OF CONSCIENCE

◆

On Becoming A Woman In The Twentieth Century And Beyond

Mary May Leach

iUniverse, Inc.
New York Lincoln Shanghai

AN EXPLORATION OF CONSCIENCE
On Becoming A Woman In The Twentieth Century And Beyond

iUniverse books may be ordered through booksellers or by contacting:

iUniverse
2021 Pine Lake Road, Suite 100
Lincoln, NE 68512
www.iuniverse.com
1-800-Authors (1-800-288-4677)

The views expressed in this work are solely those of the author and do not necessarily reflect the views of the publisher, and the publisher hereby disclaims any responsibility for them.

ISBN: 978-0-595-43634-7 (pbk)
ISBN: 978-0-595-68314-7 (cloth)
ISBN: 978-0-595-87959-5 (ebk)

Printed in the United States of America

To my late husband,
Charles Sellers Leach.
For our sons,
Jim, John, Bob, and Charlie.

Suffering is the origin of conscience
  —Fydor Dostoesevsky, *The Brothers Karamazov*

Contents

Acknowledgments

My thanks to my mother, whose faith sustained her throughout the adversity of caring for her sons and at the same time providing my education in the finest schools. I want to thank also the editors at iUniverse Publishing for their help and to Ann McCutcheon Broach for assisting me in preparing my manuscript for publication.

Foreword

When Anne Morrow Lindberg wrote her best seller, *Gifts from the Sea*, in 1955, she left home and family to sequester herself in a beach house devoid of comfort but surrounded by the visual and auditory sensations that only nature can provide in the sunrises and sunsets along the horizon of beautiful sea.

As I write this, I am not without comfort, but housed in a convenient condominium along the Gulf Shore. Perhaps, had there been condos in 1955, Mrs. Lindberg might have opted to live in such a setting while writing her book. Perhaps not. Those of us living in the latter part of the twentieth century well realize that our high-tech, affluent living is not always conducive to clear thinking. The many distractions can pollute the mind and squeeze out the subliminal thoughts derived from a life of silence, seclusion, and separation.

Introduction

Life with four sons is an encounter. With them, we have been through a period of revelation, suffered revolution, and are in a continuous stage of renewal in our old age. Throughout the mud and tears there have been many cheers to soothe many bruises. Heartaches? Some. Heartbreaks? Almost. The human heart has always been the symbol for *love*. Its beat is constant within in spite of any pounding from emotional trauma without.

A poster, placed over the kitchen stove, lingers to remind me, "Have you hugged your kid today?" It spooks me stimulating a mental collage of boys in dirty denims, athletic uniforms, clean cassocks, and graduation gowns.

In the attic, some of the old baseball mitts lie covered with cobwebs. Guitars with broken strings are stored on a shelf nearby, hoping for the touch of familiar fingers. Old musical albums, from the 1960s, a time of resistance to tradition and establishment, are stacked in boxes in the back of the closet for another generation to explore. Scouting memorabilia, music awards, sports trophies, and report cards gather dust and mildew. An orthodontic retainer and headband can be found among old posters.

The boys' rooms have been redecorated into nurseries for the grandchildren. No more pulsating beats emanating from the musical instruments in the den. No more helping with the homework. The washer and dryer are resting now in a used appliance store, replaced by new models that somehow seem out of place in the laundry room. No more baseball, football or scout uniforms to wash and dry today. No packing of lunch boxes or luggage. No stacks of dirty dishes in the sink. We traded the station wagon for a sedan and a pickup truck.

Each boy had a dog he left behind. I never for a moment considered the puppies theirs anyway. Somehow their responsibility became mine, because I allowed it to happen. Two remain, the only animate reminders of that bustling period of our family life. Even they are growing old.

1

Mothers

Mothers of diverse backgrounds, races, cultures, and religions always seem to be able to tap into an Invincible Spirit within for their strength. Their input of prayers, activated by love and fortified by hope, accesses for them the peace that sustains them day by day.

They have nurtured the uneducated hippies in the sixties, welcomed the educated yuppies of the seventies, and have tolerated their avarice and greed ever since.

They have survived the Beatles and beards, dropouts, copouts, bills, pills, minis, maxis, addictions, and suicides. "I Am Woman, Hear Me Roar," sang Helen Reddy. Yes, Helen, roar on. For those loving and learning but never leaving mothers, roar on!

During a television interview in 1987, Anne Morrow Lindberg was asked how she and her husband, Charles Lindberg, were able to bear the loss of their infant son—the pain of the horrendous kidnapping and the discovery of his tiny motionless body on the cold ground. She replied that she and her famous husband had more than their share of fame and happy experiences in their world travels as pioneers in global aviation. She said that it was through their happy experiences and sad experiences that they grew and eventually found themselves.

A mother of nine, Rose Fitzgerald Kennedy gave birth to a mentally retarded child, lost a son in World War II, lost a daughter in a plane crash, and lost two sons by assassination, one of whom was president of the United States. Later, a plethora of tragedy followed when a grandson had a leg removed because of a cancerous growth, one lost his life due to a drug overdose, another died in a skiing accident, and another in a crash of his private plane. Her daily ritual, her access mechanism, was in the attendance at Mass and recitation of the Rosary.

My own mother gave birth to two consecutive stillborn sons. They were born in the winters in Western Pennsylvania when the heavy snows prevented the only doctor in the area from traveling by horse and buggy. My father buried them in shoeboxes in the snow bank until the spring when a proper burial was possible.

Her third pregnancy resulted in the birth of a beautiful, healthy boy, who at the age of three months contracted red measles, complicated by high fever and pneumonia. The family doctor could only repeatedly plunge the little boy in ice water in hopes of reducing the soaring temperature. Convulsions followed. He was permanently brain damaged.

Following the normal births of my sister and me, another at-home prolonged birthing shortchanged the life of another baby boy. His brain damage, although not as severe, was confirmed later when he was diagnosed as "educably retarded."

Mother's faith gave her the buoyancy to transcend the awesome reality of her world. Life with her boys was an ecstasy experienced only by the mothers of the disabled.

I have witnessed the recovery of numerous close friends from the loss of their children from accidents, addictions, suicide, and epilepsy. One close friend's child was run over by a train at the age of two. They say that when you lose a child, the void and pain remain with you forever, never completely erased from memory.

Others receive their anomalies as gifts from God. With pro-life zeal, they pamper and protect their afflicted, transforming their emptiness into fulfillment. Their endurance glorifies the Creator and unlocks the secret of spiritual survival in a world without an Eden.

2

My Origin

I was born in a prosperous coalmining region of Western Pennsylvania in 1927, the daughter of a fifth generation German mother, Rose, whose father and his two brothers (John, George, and Peter Henry) were the coal barons and among the entrepreneurs of that region. They came at an early age from Bavaria.

My father's parents, my grandparents, Mary McCarthy and Patrick May, immigrated from Sligo on Donegal Bay in Ireland. They were "lace-curtain Irish" which was to be distinguished from "shanty Irish." I sensed a quiet kind of bigotry.

The Italian immigrants, as well as the majority of the Irish, were railroad workers or miners. They lived on the other side of town or across the river.

The degree of discrimination depended on the time of your arrival. The Germans were early settlers. Captain Samuel Brady rescued ancestors of mine, Margaret and Peter Henry, during the French and Indian War in 1762. Their parents had been scalped.. Peter developed agriculture interests in Butler County.[1] Captain Brady founded the community of East Brady

---

1.   See Bradys Bend Township Historical Society, Inc., *If These Hills Could Talk: A History of the Bradys Bend Township* (City: Publisher, year), 92.

in Clarion County where I was born and spent my early child-hood.

A late-coming Czechoslovakian family was readily welcomed because of their industrious nature and cleanliness. Germans truly believe that "cleanliness is next to Godliness!" There were few English and only one Jewish family. A Swede ran the bank. The Presbyterians were mostly of Scotch-Irish ancestry.

The small town, a population of about 1,200, was terraced on a hillside in the foothills of the Allegheny Mountains over-looking the Allegheny River. The historic Saint Eusebius Cath-olic Church stood on the highest ridge. Its spire could be seen for miles. Across the river, Saint Patrick's Church served the needs of the many illiterate Italians. Most spoke little or no English. Their children taught them the language as they learned it in the public school. English was necessary for all communication. It was the only acceptable language.

Beer gardens were popular and owned primarily by Italian families. I never knew why they were called gardens. They were not beautiful and they reeked of lager. A "town drunk" lived at the far end beyond the grist mill. Almost every day, he made his trek to the nearest bar, then slowly made his staggering walk home in the evening. My beloved grandmother felt so sorry for him. Any time he asked her for money, she would give him a dime. That seemed so little, but it was enough for a stein of beer!

A milkman from a nearby dairy farm, owned by the Risher family, delivered milk in in the wee hours of the morning. He placed it in insulated boxes that we kept on our door steps. The cream of the milk in glass bottles rose to the top. We did not have homogenization until the McDonald Dairy in Michigan started that process in the 1930's. The fat globules were broken up and evenly distributed.

Because of Louis Pasteur's discovery of the Germ Theory of Disease, we had pasteurized milk which eliminated the spread of typhoid fever. Dr. Pasteur's studies made medical history. He made us aware of microorganisms as the cause of disease. "Wash your hands" became and continues to be an imperative given by all mothers!

Joshua Vick, a medical doctor/pharmacist, in North Carolina in the 1900's, developed a mentholated salve, Vicks Vaporub, which was widely used for congestive problems. Its use continues today.

The main street was so much like one of Norman Rockwell's paintings. My grandfather owned the hotel. A drug store was on the same block. It sold over-the-counter medications. There were no antibiotics, no wonder drugs to prescribe. Parents relied on paregoric, a multipurpose medication for diarrhea, a cough syrup, or as an analgesic. It was camphorated tincture of opium. Its main ingredient was morphine. Some apothecaries required sign-outs. Its use declined as government stepped in to regulate it.

The cobbler occupied a dark, dismal building in which he resoled and re-heeled shoes and boots of all kinds. During the Great Depression, few could afford new shoes. We wore them until the soles wore out. Many times we slipped in cardboard until the new ones from Montgomery Ward or Sears arrived.

A liquor store stood on one corner. It was closed for a while after the owner hanged himself in the back room.

The only bank was between two large hardware stores. These were followed by a five and dime store and a men's haberdashery. The dry goods store was the biggest and most successful. Material was needed for clothing. Nearly every home had a sewing machine of some kind. Knitting needles, with skeins of colorful yarns, and spools and spools of thread were stacked on tables against the walls. Next to it was a family-owned grocery store. They had charge accounts for the needy during the Depression. Some were never paid in full.

Across the main street was the United States Post Office that held post boxes for everyone in town. My father (John Patrick May) passed the civil service exam. He served as postmaster until his death.

The only medical doctor had his small office next door. He was affectionately known as "Doc Purdom." He was compassionate and loving in his care for us. He was remembered for saying to his patients, as they left his office, "Just gimme a buck!" When he retired many years later, the community presented him with a huge dollar tree during the testimonial dinner they had for him.

It was the time when doctors made house calls. Serious cases were referred to nearby hospitals in Pittsburgh.

The Blatt Brothers, Charles, John and Bill owned the only theater. They lacked collateral for this investment. My grandfather gave them a personal check for $30,000 to begin what would become a chain of successful Blatt Brothers Theatres. He was among the few who had survived the Great Depression. In a few years, they paid the loan in full. (My grandfather's youngest daughter, Martha, married John (Jake) Blatt.)

The residential streets were lined with red maples, elms and chestnut trees.

Homes had coal bins in their basements that were kept full in preparation for the cold winters.

Perishables were kept in iceboxes. An ice man would come by weekly with an ice block. Refrigerators were not yet available on a large scale. This required lots of canning. Shelves with all kinds of canned goods, jellies, and jams lined the basement walls.

Our telephones were primitive by today's standards. We dialed only one number to reach the operator who said, "Number please." She conducted her job from a switchboard and quickly plugged in the number needed.

Beside the flourishing coal and limestone mining, the town was home to Rexhide Rubber Corporation, which moved to Texas following World War II. At this time, the coal mines were nearly depleted.

I remember vividly that my grandfather and other community leaders were happy with the status quo of their little community. They did everything in their power, including buying property, to prevent further influx of "foreigners." Sadly, these powerful men had no vision. Today, it is almost a ghost town. No industry. No mines. It is famous as the home of Jim Kelly the quarterback of the Buffalo Bills professional football team. His high school coach was Terry Henry, a cousin of mine, once removed.

Because of the Depression, few people had cars. Groceries were carried home or delivered by a family-owned market. There was no door-to-door mail delivery. A bread truck from a town nearby came to sell baked goods each week. Most people walked to their churches. (There were two Roman Catholic, one large Presbyterian, one Methodist, a small Baptist, and an evangelical "Holy Roller" group.) Our grandfather would pick us up for Mass in his big green LaSalle. My father always chose to walk.

The town's Orthodox Jew, Isadore Ackerman, and his family attended the synagogue in Pittsburgh, fifty miles away, when weather permitted. He operated the town's only taxi service. He taxied my mother and me there for intervals when I was six months old to receive radium treatments to remove a hemangioma from my "soft spot." At other times, we rode the train. The Pennsylvania Railroad was in its heyday.

His daughter, Dolores, and I were in the same grade in school. We became close friends. Our very different religious beliefs never interfered with our closeness. I felt sorry for her during the Christmas season and at Easter time. I am sure they must have celebrated Hanukkah and other religious holy days at some time, quietly, so as not to draw attention to their differentness.

From veiled ethnic bigotry evolved a noxious religious bigotry. From this new American culture, a new language was born. Its words included dago, wop, mickey, and kike. There were no blacks. We had not yet learned the word, "nigger." But the Ku Klux Klan soon came to town. We could frequently see a cross blazing on the hillside across the river at night. The WASPS (white Anglo-Saxon Protestants) were beginning to swarm.

3

Death and World War

Ten cents admission to the theatre made attendances many and frequent. The double feature on Saturday afternoon introduced us to Tom Mix, Hopalong Cassidy, Roy Rogers and Dale Evans, Gene Autry, and the Lone Ranger and Tonto. Our parents never had to question the morality of the films. The good guy and his girl, in white hats, always rode off into the sunset after getting all of the bad guys. We assumed they would live happily ever after. If only our trails in the real world could be that happy.

Newsreels preceded the feature each week. They informed us about Adolph Hitler when they covered his "Stormtroopers" in action. *TIME* magazine had displayed his picture on the front cover. The year was 1939. None of the media at that time had even hinted about the persecution of the Jews.

Our father told us when the Germans invaded Poland. We sensed his anxiety, not fully realizing how something so far across the sea could change our lives. Technology was so limited; global communication was in its infancy.

Two years later, in 1941, the year began with the sudden death of my maternal grandmother, Sophia Dickman Henry.

(My paternal grandparents died before I was born.) She died of a massive heart attack while saying the Rosary in her rocker in the kitchen by the window, where she often watched the birds as they fed in the snow. They lived next door to us in their large Victorian home, where we had celebrated their fiftieth wedding anniversary a few years before. She and my grandfather had eight children. She considered them her jewels.

My father, a compulsive worker, suffered a myocardial infarction two months later. He passed away after three weeks in intensive care at Presbyterian Hospital in Pittsburgh. He was only forty-eight years old. Cardiac care in present-day hospitals includes preventative medications, angioplasty, by-pass and open-heart surgery and even heart transplants to prolong the lives of those so afflicted. They did not exist then.

His parents had ten children. Five of them died before reaching the age of fifty from heart related problems.

I remember that he never failed to kiss us good-bye each morning. When we remained in bed as he left, he made the rounds to each of our bedrooms faithfully. When electrical storms came during our sleep in the middle of the night, he would awaken us to go downstairs to wait it out in the living room, telling us not to go near the telephone or fireplace until the lightning subsided. We gathered around our parents' bed each night during Lent while he led us in the recitation of the Rosary.

He played baseball in high school and continued that into his adulthood.

He gathered the children who lived close by on weekends to go on hikes in the surrounding hills. Later, they would play horseshoes in our side yard. His death left a huge void in the camaraderie of the neighborhood.

We listened to the radio football broadcasts with him in the fall. We sat on the floor and cut four rectangles from cardboard. These represented the four quarters of each game. We marked the yardage starting with the fifty-yard line. We drew goal posts at each end. We found, in our Crayola boxes, crayons with colors to represent the opposing teams.

We sat attentively, marking each play as the announcers gave them to us on the airwaves. Following the game, we placed the cardboards on the dining room table for a recap. This gave us the visual at a time when all we had was the broadcast on the radio. What an excellent way to learn!

Years later, when our sons played Little League baseball and high school football, I yearned for his presence. He did not live to see his grandchildren. I truly believed that he was somewhere cheering them on.

For me, at the age of thirteen, death was incomprehensible. His body was placed by the fireplace in the living room, where his chair had been removed to make way for the coffin. The wake took place over several days. Our friends and neighbors took turns bringing in food and staying up all night with mother and my father's three surviving sisters. Flowers soon filled the reception rooms. The fragrances permeated the air all over the house. Upstairs, the scent hung over our beds, filling our nostrils as we tried to rest. The noise of friends talking in the kitchen below was disturbing but comforting. We were touched by the caring and the sharing of so many. In our bitterness and grief, my sister, two brothers, and I drew strength from our mother's courage.

That same year, the Japanese attacked Pearl Harbor on December 7, 1941. We had no idea what an impact that announcement would have on our lives. We huddled around the radio to listen to President Franklin Delano Roosevelt make the declaration of war, not fully understanding what it meant or what it would do to us as a family or a community. On December 8, many of the seventeen and eighteen year old boys enlisted; some of them never returned home.

I began correspondences with relatives and friends in the armed services, never realizing how long such communication would continue. Never did I dream that it would last four years.

A cousin, serving with the Seabees on the Island of Guam in the Pacific Theater, died there during the invasion, not from battle wounds but from a ruptured appendix. No medics were available. His body was returned home after the war. His widowed mother received $10,000 from his G.I. insurance fund and a Gold Star to hang in the living room window of their home.

An uncle served with the U.S. Air Force, servicing the B-29 bombers in England. He was there at the time of the D-Day invasion of Europe. He survived. Another cousin, a medical school student, received a waiver. He did not serve in the Medical Corps until later, during the Korean War.

Rations became a reality for everyone; the war effort was top priority. Food, memorably butter and meat, were sacrificed, so was gasoline. The government issued food stamps. Factories flourished; jobs were plentiful in the production of bullets, guns, ships, and planes.

Mother and her friends joined the Red Cross and spent afternoons cutting and rolling bandages. We regularly sent "goody" boxes to boys overseas via the APO or FPO (Army and Fleet post offices). Overseas letters (V-mail) were limited in size issued by the local post offices. Censorship of all mail was mandatory because of the threat of sabotage. It wasn't easy corresponding with someone when you did not know where he was or what was happening to him and his buddies.

A year later, in 1942, my beloved maternal grandfather, John Matthias Henry, passed away. I remember how he prayed that death would take him before he became blind. His eye "ointment" was imported from Belgium; he worried about not being able to obtain it because of the war. (His younger brother was blind. Cataracts were dreaded at that time, unlike the present, when specialized ophthalmologic surgery provides cataract removal and lens implants routinely. I had cataracts removed from both eyes and received artificial implants at age sixty.) "Grandpa" took such pride in his home, which he left to his daughter, Gertrude (Gay), the only unmarried child at that time. Upon her death, the home was to be sold and divided among the heirs. He gave his many philanthropic gifts in secrecy. They were not divulged until the reading of his will and testament. One of his largest contributions was to a seminary for priests. He was a devout member of his Roman Catholic Church.

The last leaf was written in the war journal when the Japanese surrendered and the armistice was signed, in September 1945. The Allies and the Axis had buried the hatchet; now it was time to bury our dead.

The surviving sons would be coming home to their loved ones. The celebration would begin. The baby boom was on its way. A kindly pediatrician, Dr. Benjamin Spock, was busy writing his baby book, while General George Marshall wrote the Marshall Plan to restore Europe from the devastation of war. Japan remained occupied by American troops. President Truman called General Douglas MacArthur home.

Mother had placed my older brother, Jack (John Jr.), in a residential facility. There he remained until his death at the age of sixty-three. Jim, my younger brother, was classified as 4-F in the early days of the war because of his "mild" retardation. He was drafted a short while before the armistice and served with the U.S. Army Corps of Engineers. He died at the age of fifty-six in a Veteran's Hospital from complications brought on from shoveling snow. Both brothers had congestive heart failure.

4

Early Schooling

Having grade-school teachers who were not allowed to marry and were totally devoted to the art and science of education made my learning pleasurable from the beginning.

I was selected to be the director of the first-grade rhythm band. Shy little girl that I was, I played a princess in a third grade operetta. In that year, I also had to stand out in the hall for an entire period for talking when I should have been listening, which proved that there were no teacher's pets. In sixth grade, we had a terrific teacher, Mae Myers, who would tap our heads with a pencil to keep us working as she patrolled the aisles.

I had the starring role of Dorothy in a junior high production of *The Wizard of Oz*, a role that Judy Garland made famous in films. To this day, I can still sing "Over the Rainbow" on key.

My sister and I grew up in the church choir loft, but had no voice lessons. Most of our coaching came from the public school music director. She and I participated in the Pennsylvania State Forensic contests in voice each year. She always placed first. I was usually third.

Our schools did what they could to promote the arts. We learned about the classics without government grants. Our music director directed the band, glee club, and soloists. He read us stories of the operas in music class once a week. He familiarized us with the famous arias and musical scores, which we heard on his very primitive record player. How very thrilled he would be to view a DVD of *Tosca* or *Aida*. Imagine what he would think of today's mp3 players!

We recited the Pledge of Allegiance and the Lord's Prayer each morning before classes began. The Protestant children recited their full version of the prayer, the Catholic children omitted "for Thine is the Kingdom, the Power, and the Glory," and the Ackerman children were silent throughout.

There was no lunchroom and no school bus. We walked to school in the morning, back home for lunch (for some this was over a mile), returning to afternoon classes arriving home around 4:00 p.m. Glee Club, band, and sports were after-school extracurricular activities for which we received no credit.

We needed slickers and umbrellas for the rainy days, and boots, long underwear, or leggings for the snowy ones. An umbrella man came door-to-door several times each year to repair our umbrellas.

Contagious diseases were rampant, many without any control. Many died from pneumonia. The only medical doctor was held captive by bacteria and viruses for which he had no defense. A number of our friends died from poliomyelitis. It was a common sight to see an adult or child walking with a limp from its effects. This was before immunizations, penicillin, and antibiotics of any kind. God was only beginning to work through Jonas Salk for help. Sir Alexander Fleming began chemical warfare on a microscopic scale with his discovery of penicillin.

When I contracted red measles, I was homebound for a month. The Pennsylvania State Health Department nailed a quarantine notice on our front door that said, "RED MEASLES—KEEP OUT!" This was required for all contagious diseases. Upon my return to school, my teacher stayed with me after school each day until I caught up. She worked overtime, without pay, to help any child catch up who had been absent for a long period due to illness. In today's overcrowded schools, the number of absences would make it almost prohibitive for a teacher's help after school hours. Married teachers today have the responsibilities of their own families at home. Many of them are off the school grounds as soon as the children leave. Parents have to solicit help from volunteers or pay for tutoring from an outside agency.

My only sister, Patricia, a precocious child, skipped two grades, which was common at the time. She was six years older than I was, so the promotions placed her eight years ahead of me in school. That interfered with what could have been a close sibling relationship.

In contrast, our two handicapped brothers received little or no help. They sat in their classrooms, day after day, for two years without being required to do very much. I know now that along with them there had to be the non-performing dyslexics, whose potential for learning was thwarted because no one asked, "Why?" No child was diagnosed for learning gaps, and there were no prescriptive programs for them.

Diagnostic testing today gives us sophisticated tools, a complete battery of tests that affords the teacher a different perspective as she stands before her heterogeneous class. No longer is it acceptable to make every child fit the same mold. My parents found help for my younger brother in "outside" speech therapy and dance lessons to help with his motor skills.

The injuries in the school football games were common. Poorly designed helmets and faulty padding coupled with no insurance for medical expenses made the sport too dangerous. It was soon outlawed. Basketball was the only interscholastic sport, but it was for boys only. The girls were happy to participate in their intramural games. We all looked forward to Friday, when we studied the etiquette of ballroom dancing.

Discipline was enforced and the authority of the teachers was never questioned. No one chewed gum. There were no alcohol or drug problems with the students. An out-of-wedlock pregnancy was rare—and this was before birth control pills!

Condoms were around, however. We found out about them at an early age when plumbers found a wad of them bundled together, creating a stoppage in the drainage system of the unmarried minister's house. The church organist, reputed to be the community femme fatale, committed suicide a number of years later by jumping off the bridge into the Allegheny River.

She left a note requesting that her "lovers," including the minister and several local businessmen, serve as pallbearers.

Many times, when I returned from school, I would find a hobo sitting on our back steps eating a sandwich and enjoying a cup of coffee that my mother had prepared for him. We never feared the hobos. They rode railcars from town to town. This was during the Depression, and these were our street people. Sharing was a common occurrence at a time when there was little to share.

We had a constable who hung out at the firehouse whose workload was almost exclusively limited to keeping the Hardscrabble Gang, as the kids from the other end of town were called, from turning over garbage cans or writing obscenities on the sidewalks.

We sent the mentally ill to the state institutions where they were held under lock and key. We had deep compassion for those out of work; the mentally ill were ignored or ridiculed.

After-school activities included dancing in the back room of an ice cream parlor, where we could get a double scoop of ice cream for a dime and a fountain Coke for a nickel. We stayed up late at night listening to the big bands or the thriller *Inner Sanctum* on the radio. At other times, we took part in outdoor activities that nature provided—particularly in the deep snow of the surrounding hillsides, where we rode toboggans (bobsleds) eight to ten to a sled or skated on the ice of the river below.

5

The River

The wide span of the Allegheny River surrounded the town except for a small strip know as "The Narrows."

We enjoyed swimming and boating in it in the warm days of summer. We skated on its ice in the cold evenings in the winter. It was reputedly eighteen feet thick in places on the side where we lived. We built small bonfires on the top of the ice to keep warm. The blades of our skates were often so cold that touching them with bare hands meant the loss of skin. On the far side, the ice was dangerously weak where the swift current beneath eroded away the ice formation on top, creating a thin veneer ready to trap anyone brave enough to cross it.

My younger brother, Jim, and a school friend, Lonnie McCanna, both adventurous ten year olds, wandered across late one blustery afternoon. The ice gave way as they approached the bank on the far side. Both boys fell into the freezing water. An alert seventeen-year-old neighbor, Jake Klein, who was target practicing on the bank nearby, saw them and, without any consideration for his own safety, raced towards them. As he reached for my brother, the ice again gave way throwing him into the water on top of them. The weight of my brother's body and his pushed the body of the other little boy further beneath the ice.

A railroader, Hugh Morrison, heard their cries for help. He was a large man who realized that the ice would not hold his weight. He found a broken tree limb in some brush, which he feverishly dragged across the ice, using it to snag my brother's coat to lift him off the teenager's spread-eagle body that held them both. They suffered from shock and frostbite. The community suffered from the loss of a little boy whose body had gone down underneath the ice and was carried through the locks by the racing current. He was found floating by fishermen twenty miles downstream three months later, in the spring, when the ice had melted and the dogwoods bloomed. The teenager was awarded the Carnegie Medal of Honor and a scholarship for his heroism.

Schools dismissed in the spring to allow the student body and faculty to march in a group down the long hill to the riverside to watch the cascading blocks of ice that had accumulated during the meltdown in the warm air. The large drifting masses came with such strength that they carried the wooden bridge that spanned the river with them downstream while we watched in awe. We crossed the river by a ferry while the new bridge was built each year. Fortunately, engineering advances have made it possible since then to construct a stronger, higher bridge with more permanency.

The river's flow continues without any consciousness of the happy moments or tragic times it afforded us.

6

Geraldine

Throughout our lives, we develop friendships—some temporary, some lasting. Those strong ties with another individual that survive pettiness, jealousy, and differences are joyous bonds that cannot be broken even in death.

Geraldine Steele, a blue-eyed blonde with straight bobbed hair, just like me, was the very first close friend that I can remember. (Our hair remained straight in spite of the ingestion of many bread crusts that our mothers urged us to eat. I never knew whether crusts really had some magical curling power, or whether our mothers just made that up to get us to eat them.)

We were the same age. She was a Presbyterian who lived with her family down the street from us. Our birthdays were only a few days apart in April. I remember the day we got matching red shoes.

We played "paper dolls," which we cut from the magazine section of the *Pittsburgh Post Gazette* each week. We made clothes for them using the pages from old wallpaper books. It was a fantasy world. We used our imagination to design their outfits for all occasions.

When Santa Claus brought us "diadee" dolls, we were thrilled to feed them bottles of water and change their diapers. After all, we were taught that the ultimate goal for any little girl was to grow up, marry, and have children. The motivation for going to college was not necessarily for a degree but to nab a husband who had one!

We enjoyed playing "house" with any of the neighborhood kids who would join us in the old flowering lilac bush in our backyard. Its roots had spread over a large slope, creating open spaces that we called "rooms." We dreamed of having a real playhouse.

The tulips and daffodils bloomed profusely in the many flowering gardens around our area of town. The spring rains in April and warm sun in May created an explosion of flowering buds so tempting for little hands..

In our childhood innocence, on a day when there was nothing else to do, we gathered as many flowers as we could hold from the surrounding beds in the neighborhood. We tied them in bunches and sold them, door to door, for ten cents a bunch, never realizing that we had done something wrong. We were chastised by our parents, who made us apologize to the neighbors whose flowerbeds we had stripped. Any further thought of continuing what could have been a profitable partnership was "nipped in the bud!"

We had fun beneath the high back porch of the large frame house where Geraldine lived. We gathered corn silks from her father's large garden in the backyard, wrapped them in thin sheets of paper, and smoked our "cigarettes" in the crawl space, which we reached through an opening in one end of the porch foundation.

We searched for the wild huckleberries and elderberries that grew on the mountainside in early summer. Numerous fruit trees in our backyards provided us with snacks before the picking in the harvest for canning and making jellies. Geraldine and I liked the large red cherries best. Stomachaches were common.

In our last summer together, Geraldine had a serious gastronomical attack accompanied by a high fever. Her mother gave her a laxative, a common cure for the time for stomach ailments, which caused her swollen appendix to rupture. Cherry pits had lodged there, creating the fiery inflammation. The local doctor, always helpless with no curing medication, prepared us for the ugly peritonitis that followed. She died a week later at the age of ten.

There was no funeral parlor in the small town. My parents accompanied me to the wake in her family home. I was pleased that my father had purchased red roses for her pall. Sadness stayed with me a very long time.

Geraldine, wherever you are, I still love you!

7

The Convent School

I was enrolled in a Catholic convent school for girls, Villa Maria Academy in Erie, Pennsylvania, one hundred miles away. I was not prepared for the strict environment, but I will be forever grateful for those dear nuns, their demand for excellence and instillation of values so necessary for women of all ages.

They taught us the fear of God and the love of Christ. The fear, I suppose, was to scare the hell out of us. Like all astute students of Catholicism, we studied the *Towering Inferno* by Dante (thirteenth century) and memorized his famous warning: "The hottest places in Hell are reserved for those who, in time of moral crisis, remain neutral."

I do not know of any physical punishment, nor do I remember any girl going to the office for chastisement. We knew what the sisters expected of us. We changed classes single file, in silence. We stood when called upon in class.

Each class began with prayer in unison, in English; if the class was a foreign language class, we prayed in that language. I can still pray in Latin and Spanish.

The pews in the chapel where we attended Mass fit only two, creating a number of aisles. One nun was always assigned the

31

duty of walking up and down the aisles to make certain that we didn't slouch. I received a nudge or two several times. Praying in the morning was not difficult, but maintaining good posture was. The dear sisters reminded us that God deserved open eyes and an erect body.

In guidance class, we learned a lot about chastity and charity. We were taught that our bodies house Divine life and that sex was the privilege of married people. Nothing was said about pregnancy, how to avoid it or how to terminate it. Abstinence was stressed.

Our school uniforms were navy blue with starched white collars and white cuffs that fastened at the end of the long sleeves, nothing like the pretty blazers and colorful plaid skirts the students wear today. The dear sisters wore habits, which identified them anywhere. Black rosaries hung from their sides. We wondered about their hair. Was it short? Did they shave their heads? Today, few orders require habits. I miss that period, when the mere sight of a habit immediately commanded respect. Often progress develops towards the secular and we miss the point of the power derived from the spiritual.

World War II continued with our involvement in Europe with Germany and Italy. Battles in the Pacific Theater with Japan were fierce as we tried to recapture the control of vital islands in the vast sea. It was the Allies (United States, Great Britain, France, and Russia) vs. the Axis (Japan, Germany, and Italy), with our president telling us that we had nothing to fear but fear itself. The prime minister of England, Winston

Churchill, told the people of his war-weary land that all they needed to win the war was their blood, sweat, and tears.

We all knew a lot about "Ike," General Dwight David Eisenhower, who was named Supreme Allied Commander in charge of the European Theater of Operations. Army Chief of Staff George Marshall was the overseer from his post in Washington, D.C. Leading troops in North Africa and Europe were Generals Omar Bradley and George Patton. General Lord Mountbatten's genius gave England its hand in the operation.

Admirals Bull Halsey, King, and Spruance held together the Pacific Fleet. With their help, General Douglas MacArthur, U.S. Army, led his men in invasions; when they lost the battle of the Philippines, he said, "I shall return!" And he did!

Some of the new words added to our language, knowledge acquired from the war, were Nazi, Jap, Axis, Allies, U-boat, PT-boat, B-29, A-1, A-f, WAC, WAVE, V-Mail, kamikaze, hari-kari, atom bomb, and holocaust.

No one complained. We were united in a common cause.

The only disgraceful sign of a still very segregated society in our armed forces was our bigotry against blacks. Black sons could not associate with our white sons although the uniforms and their mission were the same. When they were killed in battle, their mothers received gold stars to hang in their windows, too.

As always, music sustained us. Irving Berlin composed "God Bless America," into which Kate Smith poured her heart and soul. Juke boxes and home radios played sentimental songs. "I

Walk Alone," "Don't Sit Under The Apple Tree With Anyone Else But Me," and "Coming In On A Wing And A Prayer" became theme songs for our boys on all fronts. Girls danced with other girls. There was no thought of lesbianism during this time. We were proud to be Americans.

One beautiful June morning in 1944, we could hear newsboys out on the streets yelling, "D-Day, D-Day! Europe Invasion Begun!" General Eisenhower and the Allies had been waiting for the right weather conditions to embark. The day we all had been waiting for had finally come! It was a long time before we realized that over 10,000 boys had been lost in the operation. Omaha Beach will long be remembered for the blood shed there. A war to end all wars was taking many lives, but our victory in Europe was just around the corner. General George Patton was on his way. The atom bomb was in the hangar. Japan, too, would soon fall.

Nearly a year later, on April 12, 1945, my senior classmates and I were attending a concert given by Phil Spitalny and his All-Girl Orchestra. (I suppose the group was organized because of the lack of boys. One does not hear of all-girl orchestras anymore.) The music was interrupted by an announcement of the death of President Roosevelt. (He was a victim of polio, confined to a wheel chair most of his adult life.) The theater was silenced, and people left weeping.

Our graduation ceremony had all the pomp and circumstance of Catholic Church functions. Bishop John Mark Gannon, soon thereafter to be archbishop, gave us our diplomas.

The entire class was attired in long white evening gowns—long sleeved; no décolleté for us! Each carried one dozen long-stemmed red roses. This complemented the bishop's scarlet robe as we sat on the large stage with his chair in the middle at the highest tier. It was great theater!

The surrender of Germany followed in May 1945. The transition of power was swift, as Harry Truman, the little man from Missouri, who had served as vice president, took office. What a burden to be placed on his shoulders!

The final blow to the Japanese came when he issued the order for the use of the atomic bomb on August 6, 1945. Lt. Col. Paul Tibbetts had the awesome task of piloting the plane that carried the bomb. Tom Ferebee was bombardier.

The venom from that blast would live in the survivors and heirs for generations.

Five days later, World War II came to a close.

8

Higher Education

An older cousin, Wilbur Wallace, attended the University of Michigan in Ann Arbor. He later became the physician for the city schools. It was his influence that convinced me to enroll in the University of Michigan School of Nursing.

There, I aced organic chemistry (an impossibility today) and was failing nursing arts, which included bathing a patient and shampooing a patient's hair in bed. Those were the days when every nurse on the floor was an RN. We had no LPNs, no aides. Nurses were required to have their hair off their collars, and wear white uniforms and shoes. Each wore a cap uniquely designed which identified the hospital where she received her training. Antibiotics had not been discovered, so every room had to be aseptically clean!

Our class was fortunate to have our studies with pre-medical school students in anatomy and physiology on human cadavers. Six students, nursing and pre-meds, were assigned to two bodies. I was with a group that studied on an eighteen-year-old girl who died from tuberculosis and an aging miner who died from black lung disease. They were preserved in formaldehyde.

Adjusting to the bodies was not a problem for us, but the strong odor of the preservative made the study difficult. Our lab was before lunch at the university hospital. Needless to say, we had no desire for food.

All organs, veins, arteries, and nerves were tagged. We were taught to respect the cadavers, which had stamped in blue on their backs, "Donated to the University of Michigan Medical School." Along with the usual bluebook, we were required to identify each part tagged and define its use.

Following capping ceremonies, I completed my education in medical technology. Working with Johns Hopkins University internists after graduation proved to be valuable to my education. Medical therapy was advancing apace.

Present-day labs are "computerized," with machines doing the readouts, unlike in our day, when we collected blood samples, made filtrates in the morning, and "cooked" them in the afternoon to be read by a colorimeter. We developed electrocardiograms in a dark room. We determined heart sizes on a fluoroscope by orthodiagraphic tracings.

Dormitories were single sex. Girls had to sign out and in before 10 p.m. Students were forbidden to ride in cars on campus. We walked to classes in all kinds of weather. The winter snows in Michigan did not preclude attendance. We walked to the weekend dances and later to the formal balls in the spring—all while dressed in long gowns and high heels!

The university was multicultural then, as it is today. Yet few blacks attended. We had an all-white football team. My dorm housed girls from the Philippines whose families had been abused by the Japanese during their occupation. The girls revered Americans, but they always carried cans of Lysol to the dormitory's community bathroom. They had heard that American girls were promiscuous and felt that the disinfectant spray protected them! They returned to their homeland as registered pharmacists.

The daughter of the Ecuadorian ambassador to England provided us with lots of information about the customs of her country. She and her brother radioed their parents from Detroit. TV and cell phones did not yet exist.

An Asian-Indian "princess," who wore a genuine ruby in her forehead, added mystique with her religious beliefs. As a Hindu, she was permitted to bathe only in naturally running waters. We were delighted when the waters of the Washtenaw River around Ann Arbor thawed in the warm weather of the spring.

We became acquainted with Chinese male students who worked in the grill close to our dorm on campus. We took turns on trips to the grill for burgers for take-outs late at night when studying for exams. No Chinese cuisine was served. They were making a transition to our American food and lifestyle.

The annual ritual in the spring with the university approval was the "panty raid," carried out by the boys' fraternities on the girls' dormitories. We tossed our "undies" out the windows as wild exclamations from the raiders signaled their catches. I often wondered what they did with them—the whole ritual seemed so perverse. Undoubtedly, it was their way to break the monotony of a restrictive environment.

My only disconcerting experience regarding my religious beliefs was in a lecture conducted by a European history professor. While studying the Protestant Reformation, we were taught about all of the abuses by the Roman Catholic Church, abuses I had never heard of or was never made aware of in my education at a prominent Catholic girls' school. My parents had never discussed it.

When I confronted him after class about the church's practice of selling indulgences, he could sense my indifference. His only comment was that if I wanted to pass the course, I had better answer any pertinent questions in the bluebook according to his valid instruction.

Today, I remain a practicing Catholic, although I am sometimes cynical because of the effort of some in the church, who teach only what is good about Roman Catholicism. I realize that the good works of the present prevail and surpass much of the malice of the past. I have learned from this that cover-ups can occur in any organization, which should alert us to search for discrepancies. I hope that my sons will always respect authority but never fear to question it.

9

The Right One in the Right Place at the Right Time

During WWII, the U.S. Naval Academy was not large enough to fulfill the demand for officers. The academy took over Milligan College in Johnson City, Tennessee, where they brought in scholarship students from all parts of the country for basic training. After two years, they were dispersed. Some were sent to Harvard, Yale, Notre Dame, the Universities of Michigan, Minnesota, Wisconsin, and other illustrious colleges to complete their educations and receive their commissions in the regular navy as those graduating from the Academy at Annapolis, Maryland.

While attending the university, I met my husband, who was in the navy training group. He was two years ahead of me. The university was on a wartime schedule when completing studies for a degree was condensed into a three-year period. We had five days off for Christmas and four for spring break—*period!*

It came as no surprise when he was accepted in the famous University of Michigan Marching Band, under the leadership of William Revelli. He was selected to play first chair, first trombone. (I do not know at what age he was given a trombone, but I do know that his mother paid him seventy-five cents per week to practice. That was in the forties, when seventy-five cents was worth a lot more than in the present day. Friends who grew up on the same street attested to his faithfulness in practicing. They could hear him! He formed an orchestra in high school that played for school dances and honkytonks close by.)

He received his commission in the regular navy upon graduation and immediately went to sea.

We married two years later, in 1949, in the student chapel on the campus of the university, and we honeymooned in Canada. We stayed at a manor overlooking Lake Ontario that had Japanese interns in its employ. This was the first experience we had with the situation and felt an easiness about our country's and Canada's decision to treat them in such a fashion.

We began our union, as so many of our generation had, as a navy career couple, understanding that separation would be frequent and challenging.

He served on the USS *Tarawa* before transferring to "The Mighty Warrior," the USS *Coral Sea*. It was among the largest active-duty warships, which have since been replaced by nuclear-powered vessels. His tour of duty in the Pacific continued after the war.

While serving on the USS *Tarawa* and USS *Coral Sea*, he sought out other musicians to form small orchestras for the enjoyment of those on board and so far away from home.

Upon his return to place the ship in dry dock at Portsmouth, Virginia, we found an apartment close to the naval base furnished at $40 a month! Other officers and their wives chose upscale apartments, but we decided to save money while toughing it out!

He spent every fourth night on board. Fortunately for him, he ate in the officers' mess, which included steak for breakfast. I knew how to boil water and poach an egg. I still have the cookbook my mother gave me, splattered and tattered in a drawer with updated recipes. I improved my education in the kitchen with the birth of each boy. They will tell you that over the years I have mastered the art of cuisine—out of necessity!

One of the highlights of my stay in Portsmouth was the privilege to enjoy dinner on Saturday evenings on board the carrier in the captain's mess. The massive structure was awesome, and the many flights of stairs one had to maneuver downward was exhausting as we descended into the spacious dining room. Glass cases of the ship's silver services around us gleamed and were surpassed only by the spit and polish of everything in the room. Blacks in white coats served us. There were no black officers on board.

His tour of duty in the Pacific continued after the war. Going to sea on a carrier around the world included the evacuation of Americans from Red China in 1948. My husband was in the naval task force that rescued thousands. Among those was my first cousin, Sister Patricia Maria Jackson, a missionary nun who was teaching in Tsingtao.

Years later, in 1979, they had a reunion following my mother's funeral in Pennsylvania. Presently, she is residing in the Mother House of the Sisters of Saint Joseph in Baden, Pennsylvania. She is ninety-four years old.

10

The South, 1950

We returned to my husband's roots in Tennessee when he completed his tour of duty. He went into the Naval Reserve and served as commanding officer of the U.S. naval unit in Paducah, Kentucky, until his retirement twenty years later.

I was overwhelmed by the warmth and friendliness extended to me, a transplanted Catholic Yankee, from my husband's family and friends. I was a pioneer in foreign territory. I not only had an accent that might have seemed harsh in comparison to the slow Southern drawl, but I didn't know what soul food was, let alone how to cook it, and I went to the wrong church! Little did I realize what they believed about Catholics. Little did I know about the subtle hostility breeding in this new environment.

My encounter with blacks—or "nigras" as they were called—was nil. I had not seen a black person or anyone of color until I was thirteen years old. (The small town where I grew up in Pennsylvania had no blacks and still has none today.) When I approached the ladies' room in a public building, I was amazed to find COLORED and WHITE over the entries. There were similar signs over the drinking fountains.

The Civic Auditorium was the center for culture and entertainment. When attending a concert there for the first time, I noticed a rope sectioning off a portion of the large hall. I asked if this was for local dignitaries. My naiveté was showing. I registered dismay when I was told that it served to contain the blacks! We enjoyed minstrels there until desegregation was enforced. It is no longer permitted to blacken faces of the entertainers in ridicule or to rope anyone off from sitting where they choose.

The auditorium today, in its antiquity, has been restored. Once a center of amusement for a bigoted culture, it now houses a center for the handicapped of all races.

My in-laws, Ruth Evans and Wendell Clifford Leach, were sixteen years apart in age, very conservative, and very discriminating. They considered blacks inferior and Northerners (Yankees) undesirable. Neither experienced growth in their perception, possibly due to limited travel and socialization with others in different parts of the country or the world. The Civil War, which pitted brother against brother, had a lingering bitter effect.

He was a proud Methodist whose first wife had died in childbirth. He had two grown children from that marriage and had adopted my husband at the age of two. (His biological father had abandoned him.) Because of her divorce, his mother was no longer permitted to attend the church of her birth, the Church of Christ. Their marriage was a success in every way. My husband's stepfather passed on his business acumen to him and was partly responsible for our later success in a music enterprise.

In the post—World War II days, business was booming. Couples dressed in their finery to attend progressive dinner parties in the small town in Tennessee where they lived. My in-laws were active in socializing always in dining and playing bridge. The town had innumerable bridge clubs that often had large competitive parties. The women always wore hats and gloves.

At home, meals were served on a linen tablecloth, in the dining room. They had a young black man, whom they called their "house boy," to clean the house and take care of the yard. Because they did not have a washer and dryer, they sent linens to the local laundry weekly. My mother-in-law was known for her Southern cooking that always included butter and whipped cream. Homemade dinner rolls were a specialty of hers.

In retrospect, I mourn the passing of that era. Lifestyles have changed in the Old South. Rarely do you see a man stand when a woman enters the room. When the housewife left home to become a breadwinner and compete in the world, she lost the respect once afforded her. As an equal, she remains a challenge in the workplace.

"Yes, ma'am" and "Yes, sir" are seldom heard. "Hey, you!" has replaced "Pardon me." With all the madness to get ahead, we now have road rage on our highways, which exemplifies the loss of gentility and manners that we once appreciated.

(My father-in-law, known affectionately by our family as "Pop Leach," died in the late sixties. He had developed Alzheimer's, but lived at home until he passed away with heart failure in his eighties. My mother-in-law succumbed to congestive heart failure in the early seventies. She was sixty-four years old. This was one week before our local hospital began cardiac monitoring. Surgery of any kind had not yet begun.)

11

Hillcrest Circle

When Dwight Eisenhower became President, we saw the mass production of cars, and the construction of interstate highways. Kemmons Wilson began his chain of Holiday Inns, McDonald's opened drive-ins, and America was on the road for the first time since the war.

Following the return of World War II veterans, the baby boom created a demand for new housing. Architects designed the one-story "ranch house" for the suburbs and the scramble began. The government offered loans under the G.I. Bill for college education and/or housing for those who served making housing accessible.

A local distinguished bank president, Mississippi bred with a keen knowledge of what was desperately needed, opened the orchard of eighteen acres behind his home, dividing it into ten lots with the idea of selling them to buyers by "invitation only." We were honored that we were included in the select number.

There were no regulations other than the houses had to be above $8,000 in building costs. The lots were $1,500. A variety of homes were built, no two alike. They were simple in design but adequate for each family, with nothing like the square footage and extravagance of homes being built today.

We were prolific. The small circle within a few years produced nineteen children, with as many dogs. One of the fathers created a list of rules for the children, demanding that if they needed to use the bathroom or get a drink, they had to go home. When they returned for lunch, each stayed there until 3 p.m.!

All of the mothers were stay-at-home moms; dads came home for lunch. Each family had only one car. That necessitated carpooling to school and after-school activities.

It was typically an "Ozzie and Harriet" neighborhood. But it was not, as Hollywood might depict, free of challenges and startling adversities. Through the years, the families faced innumerable illnesses, which makes one question how or why they could develop in such a small cul-de-sac. In the group of ten homes, the contagious diseases of childhood spread, at times from house to house. A few of the homes had more serious illnesses, ending in death—one by suicide, another from epileptic seizure. Bipolar disorders, anorexia, and paranoid schizophrenia surfaced in families completely unaware of the existence of such genes in their medical histories.

Genetic studies were advancing; professional help was available. We were in the beginning stages of understanding the causes of the problems.

Discoveries in mental health and neurology in the latter part of the 20th Century have created a sophisticated attitude toward treatment.

It was the sixties. I am sure that most of the children, then college age, experimented with marijuana. Fortunately, none of them today are addicts.

We were an ecumenical group of parents who believed in the power of prayer and resignation to God's will.

Although many of the children's marriages ended in divorce, all the parents have remained married. Most have reached their fiftieth anniversaries and beyond.

12

Our Early Family Life

We produced two boys in a ten-month period. As a new mother, I did extremely well with them, and they were good babies. Eight years later, I gave birth to another boy, followed by another two years after that. They had colic for months! It was a difficult time for me. The older boys were then in school and I was taking part in PTA duties and had become a Cub Scout den mother.

Dr. Benjamin Spock's baby book saved my days! The yellowed first publication was handed down to the parents of our first-born grandchild. He told us to let our babies advance at their own rate. Today, there are standardized charts to follow their early development. Experts tell us when they should roll over, sit up, talk, walk, and be potty trained. This only creates anxiety in mothers and threatens fathers. We cannot induce readiness.

One son did not talk in sentences until he was twenty months old. This was a signal of his perceptual developmental delay. Problems did not surface until he started school. His first-grade teacher told us to let him progress at his own rate. Wrong! They should have told us to find the reason for his developmental delay. He made it through elementary school somehow, until he developed headaches in the sixth grade. These were so serious that he required a homebound teacher to help him with his reading. You must understand that, at this time, no one was aware that dyslexia existed.

The family physician sent us to LeBonheur Children's Hospital in Memphis, where he was seen by seven pediatricians of various specialties. He was hospitalized there for a week. We came home without finding any cause. Teachers in the seventh grade consistently compared him to his two older brothers, who had no problems. We consulted the school reading specialist, who told us that he was reading grade level with an IQ of 130! This was well below his expectancy. When we told her that he was disturbed about his reading, she suggested "emotional problems" and referred us to a child psychiatrist. After completing a thorough examination of our son, the psychiatrist told us that he did have an emotional problem that could be resolved through "appropriate education," whatever that meant.

As we reached out for the best professional help, everyone, including his grandparents, said that nothing was wrong with him. We *knew* there was nothing wrong with him. He had no problem until he started school.

Conclusion: there must be something wrong with the school!

On our own, without consulting anyone else, we made an appointment for an eye exam with a local optometrist. He called us to say that his vision was okay, but he definitely had a perceptual problem, whatever that meant.

Fortunately, for him and us, we learned that the University of Alabama Medical School had begun, in its psychology department, research on *perceptual*-motor problems causing reading disorders in bright children. We immediately enrolled him in their intensified reading program. As a result, he has become a very successful businessman.

Charles L. Shedd, Ph.D., psychology department, University of Alabama Medical School, Birmingham, Alabama, began his research in the early 1970s by establishing non-profit tutorial programs (over 200) in the Southeast to prove that the APSL—the alphabetic, phonetic, structured, linguistic material—worked. It was multisensory, much like the proven Orton-Gillingham method, but more practical and affordable. Hiring professionals at $50 per hour was not feasible or far-reaching enough.

I began as program director in a small community in Northwest Tennessee in 1971. Dr. Shedd and his staff came in for evaluations twice a year and did follow-up read-outs to measure gains. Meanwhile, we trained mothers and other para-educational personnel in the materials and methodology. Our gains were phenomenal.

The term, dyslexia, was first coined by a Dr. Berlin in Germany in 1887. This was derived from the Greek meaning difficulty with letters or language. Difficulty with mathematic symbols was called dyscalculia. In Europe, strephosymbolia, meaning scrambled symbols, was another terminology. Today we have learned that the problem encompasses far more than just scrambling alphabetic or mathematic symbols.

In the early 1900s, the World Federation of Neurologists, led by Dr. MacDonald Critchley, in London, England, opened the Word Blind Institute for those with reading difficulty, while Dr. Sam Orton and his colleague, Anna Gillingham, were developing the Orton-Gillingham method for teaching these children in the United States. This was structured and multisensory incorporating vision, audition, tactation, and kinesthesis. Now we have multiple methods of teaching for remediation recognized by IMSLEC, the International Multisensory Structured Educational Council in Dallas, Texas.

The work conducted by Dr. Charles Shedd provided data along with data from hundreds of programs throughout the country to prove that these children could be taught to read to their expectancy.

As a program director of a tutorial program operating outside of the public schools, neither I nor the program was received with open arms. We were able to teach children that public schools could not and we were doing it non-profit as a parent-cooperative. The federal government got into the act in 1975–76, when Congress passed the bill for the handicapped, Public Law 94-142. But it was not funded. Help for these children was demanded in public schools, which had no money to train teachers in multisensory teaching, no money for tutors.

Some parents chose to sue the school; others who could afford it sent theirs to private schools. The poor, as always, got nothing. I wonder how many of our street people, the school dropouts, are undiagnosed dyslexics who would have been productive if given the appropriate education.

I continued to work in the tutorial program because there were so many mothers who truly cried for help.

Early on, the disciplines were very competitive. The allergists believed that coloring and preservatives in food were the culprits. Then came the optometrists with their special lenses and the pediatricians with their medications for controlling behavior. Speech and hearing specialists were on the sidelines. To some degree, all are right. Today, the specialty advancing apace is neuropsychology.

I am one of the lucky ones. I found help early for my child. Because of that, I have met hundreds of mothers and appreciated their love and friendship. Nothing has changed since I was first introduced to the world of dyslexia. After all the research, much of which is going on as I write this, and after all the thousands of how-to and help books, mothers continue to mourn while their children become casualties of school systems that do not work for them.

The annual conferences of the International Dyslexia Association are held throughout the United States and abroad. These are helpful in providing information for parents, teachers and Medical professionals. Information can be obtained by calling toll-free 1-800-ABC-D123, the office of the association in Maryland.

13

The International Dyslexia Association

The nomenclature surrounding dyslexia (knowing what to call bright children who had difficulty reading or calculating) got in the way of figuring out what to do about it. Early on, any professional declaring the existence of such learning disorders was quickly shunned. Waiting for the data, was accumulating throughout the country, took time. Meanwhile, the children with such learning disabilities suffered.

The only reputable organization was the Orton Society, named for Dr. Sam Orton, one of the pioneers in the study. It was comprised of somewhat pompous individuals who charged exorbitant fees for tutoring. I felt a sense of self-aggrandizement surfacing. Their conferences were all about the Orton-Gillingham Method, the only method known, in the early seventies to get good results.

Dr. Orton once told his followers to look for the proficiency when there is a deficiency. This stands as good advice today. The theory of multiple intelligences is gaining ground.

Dr. Mel Levine, presently (2006) at the University of North Carolina Medical School, is one of the leaders in the field to support this. Everyone has a niche. Finding that is not always easy. This is an educational puzzle that needs desperately the intervention of medical professionals to help with the understanding of the problem.

Beth Israel Hospital, Boston; Columbia Presbyterian Hospital, New York; Johns Hopkins University Medical School, Baltimore; Mayo Clinic, Minneapolis; Vanderbilt University, Nashville; and LeBonheur Children's Medical Center, Memphis are several that offer the finest neurological assessments available. But these are not accessible for the average family.

The Orton Society became the International Dyslexia Association in the 1980s. It needed growth and new blood. Although I had attended regularly their annual conferences, I did not join until 1998. Harley Tomey, president, and Tom Viall, executive director, of IDA in Bethesda, Maryland, came to Tennessee at that time to establish our state organization. I was honored to become a member of its founding board.

We are strengthened by the opening of the Center for Dyslexia Studies at Middle Tennessee State University in Murfreesboro, Tennessee. It is state funded, under the direction of Dr. Diane Sawyer.

The federal government under President George W. Bush has intervened with the passage of the "No Child Left Behind" Act to legislate accountability. The further these children go, the further behind they get. Emotions get out of control at home and in the classroom. Hormones kick in. Welcome to puberty! If this legislation fails, more and more children will end up in alternative schools. Even worse, they may end up in our jails and on our streets.

14

Music, Music, Music

After settling in with his navy duties and getting accustomed to frequent inspections by the admiral from Atlanta, Georgia, my husband again pursued his career in music by opening a music store. My help included decorating the windows and keeping books.

He contacted the band directors of area high schools and colleges to form a ten-piece orchestra, The Aristocrats. They accepted engagements in a quad-state area playing for proms, wedding receptions, and celebrity functions.

He started a recording company with the label, Four Sons Recording Company. It was a time when "45" records were in demand.

The music store prospered in the advent of The Beatles and many other similar groups. Guitars replaced the upright and grand pianos, which we moved to another room in the store. At first, there were "flat tops." The electrical guitars followed with need for amplifiers.

The Elvis craze continued." Rhythm and blues" records were reserved under the counter for our black customers. When my husband came home one evening, he revealed with complete shock that white students were buying rhythm and blues records. He remarked that this was truly a culture shift. He was so right! It was just the beginning.

All four of our sons were musically oriented. The oldest played first chair, first trumpet in the high school band. The second son played clarinet and guitar. The third and fourth sons also chose guitar. The youngest (our fourth) became our only pianist.

Our older sons joined a group named The Counts. They played for school dances and entered the Mid-South Talent Contest at the County Fair in Memphis. Winning first place was exciting. Their reward consisted of a trip to New York to be on the "Ted Mack Amateur Hour." That resulted in job offers around the country. Because college careers lay ahead, they declined. Their father and I were pleased about that.

As the Big Band era declined, so did the demand for the dances so popular in the forties and fifties. Ballroom dancing, even jitterbugging, became passé. Bluegrass music was revived, and rock and roll was "in."

When attending any reunion, we would find someone trying to contact "the boy" who could play the trombone by ear. They nearly always wanted him to play the songs made famous by other trombonists well known in the Big Band era, namely, Tommy Dorsey and Glenn Miller.

Before long, he was contacted by a new director of the Jackson Symphony Orchestra, in Jackson, Tennessee, Dr. Jordan Tang, who was looking for a trombonist. Their schedule was demanding, weekly practice mandatory. I learned so much about classical music from him in this new adventure.

15

Discrimination/Integration

We engaged a middle-aged black woman as a weekly maid, known at the time as "household he'p" when our firstborn arrived.

She cleaned the house in the morning and ironed in the afternoon for $2 per day. This was before permanent press material. Shirts had to be starched, and there were lots of shirts!

(Minimum wage laws and Social Security regulations now protect the household employees.)

She lived in a black section of town, where the houses were run down, patched, and squalid. It hasn't changed in fifty years, although the cars are bigger and TV antennae are taller.

When a shiftless black escaped from the local jail, he was reported to be in a house on her street. Police forced their way into each house, rummaging through closets in a harsh invasion of privacy that startled the tenants and their small children. It was conducted without search warrants. The illiterate blacks did not know to ask about them. They must have realized that lack of education, not being able to read with proficiency, was an impediment to progress and civil rights.

Another black man helped on our farm in the country. My husband gave him a list of chores each morning. It wasn't until he was admitted to a nursing home many years later that we found out he could not read. He had taken the chore list each morning to a nephew to read for him the entire time he worked for us.

Language communication problems still exist. Literacy programs after high school struggle to teach reading to those dysfunctional in decoding the printed word. Without reading proficiency, no country can hope to eradicate poverty. There will always be those who cannot qualify for decent jobs and decent housing. With little comprehension of the written word, how can they understand personal hygiene or steps necessary for good health?

I have always said, "Everything goes back to reading"; my husband would qualify this by saying, "No, everything goes back to money!"

We saw President Eisenhower order the National Guard to Arkansas to enforce integration. Governor George Wallace defied the Federal Court order until troops went to Alabama to redirect his thinking. His state attorney general's son, Richmond Flowers, refused a football scholarship to the University of Alabama because black boys were prevented from playing on its all-white team. Richmond went on to play for the University of Tennessee as a standout. A movie, *The Richmond Flowers Story* was produced about his courage in his conscientious objection to such injustice.

The assassinations of President John F. Kennedy, the Reverend Martin Luther King, and Bobby Kennedy gave credence to the bias still alive in our free country. Later, we would see President Gerald Ford and President Ronald Reagan escape fatal bullets in assassination attempts.

When our schools were integrated in 1968, snide remarks and hidden prejudices surfaced.

I remember when a black girl, a student at the high school, called our home one evening to get an assignment from our oldest son. Not knowing the reason for the phone call, I came apart and cried. I discovered that I, too, a mother who had preached equality to her children, had an intolerance that I did not know I had. Class bias? Class hatred? Surely not.

There were further tests, and I suppose there will always be, of this new racial consciousness. At a high school football game, I followed our band members (all four sons were/are musicians) into the stadium and noticed that a black student had dropped his music. The white students offered no help. As they came to the scattered sheets of music, they ground them into the gravel and mud with the heels of their shoes. I was shocked.

After classes one afternoon, I saw a white girl from a prominent family get into a car with four black boys. I was appalled.

Ambivalent feelings. Two minds. Was this slowly surfacing prejudice inherent in me? I soon learned that black mothers were having as much difficulty with their feelings. When our sons and several other white boys invited a black classmate to go with them to a basketball game, we hesitatingly approved.

Upon arrival at his home in Black Bottom, his mother invited them in and asked them to sit down to talk. Her judgment was sound. She thanked them for their courtesy in inviting him but went on to explain to them the problems they would have if they sat together at the game. She said that folks were not ready to accept them, even though it was legal to do so.

They went to the game without him.

16

Decisions about Mother

My only sister and I seldom agree on anything. We agree on Billy Graham, the Baptist evangelist, whose beliefs, conveyed on regular TV broadcasts, are extremely sincere. He is truly a prophet!

When our widowed mother's health was failing in the 1970s, we agreed to close the family home and care for her individually for six months at a time. That meant six months in Pennsylvania in the spring and summer and six months of winter in Tennessee. We agreed that we wanted to do something *for* her and refrained from saying, "What are we going to do *with* her?"

She loved the idea of flying. Her small form and gray hair was reminiscent of the late actress Helen Hayes when she starred in the film *Airport*. She was feisty and comfortable in the close surroundings of the plane. At that time, champagne was always offered. She refused, only because she did not want to miss any view out of her window seat—imbibing would have made her sleepy. Clouds represented heaven to her, and she was awed by how small everything on Earth appeared, how insignificant everything looked from a faraway perspective.

We enjoyed her company. Any time I became upset about something, she would say, "Look what you are doing to yourself!" She was a smoker who always followed that remark with "You would be a nicer person if you had a cigarette once in a while!"

As a daughter of an affluent family in the early twentieth century, she, as well as her five sisters, received only a high school education. Her two brothers went to colleges close by. This was the custom of that period. Only boys, the future breadwinners, needed higher education. The girls would be homemakers and mothers.

Mother's intelligence was impressive. Not only did she excel in math and English, but she was an accomplished pianist. Girls were expected to take piano lessons. She was exceptional in spelling, learning to spell phonetically and with ease of syllabication. In her later years, she corresponded with innumerable friends and nieces. Along with a bed, she always needed a writing desk.

She told me that the best way to determine if you really loved a boy was to ask yourself if you could wash his underwear out by hand. In her day, they washed clothes on a washboard!

Another gem of hers was that it was important not to talk about anyone who might seem odd or difficult. She explained that there is always a reason why people are the way they are.

Her acceptance of the adversity in her life was strengthened by her doubtless faith. Mother's grief never surfaced. Her love of people and her genuine kindness are remembered by those who knew her intimately. What an example she was for me!

When we moved to the farm, she reveled in walking in the pasture near our Charolais cattle. Country life was so new to her. We drove her several miles south to see the cotton fields. She plucked branches to bring home for her room, as well as some to send to her Pennsylvania friends.

She watched the *Lawrence Welk Show* religiously and could tell you the names of everyone in his orchestra.

She lived to see her firstborn grandson graduate from medical school (University of Tennessee Health Sciences in Memphis). She had lost four sons. She cherished ours.

On her last visit to Tennessee, she had a severe stroke, which necessitated placing her in a facility not far from our home. She was unable to speak and was paralyzed on one side. I cried each time I saw her. Remembering how much she liked orange sherbet, I would feed her a cup while praying aloud parts of the Rosary, which was her special form of daily prayers.

She weighed ninety-eight pounds when she married and ninety-eight pounds when she died at the age of eighty-four. A crushing loss.

My husband and I flew home to Pennsylvania with her body to bury her in the family plot next to my father and my brothers. My sister and I were lectors at the funeral Mass, which was celebrated by our close first cousin, Father Thomas Jackson of Pittsburgh.

There are so many ways to interpret the hereafter. No one has ever been there and returned to tell us about it. I believe that in another dimension the spirits of our loved ones remain with us. I am comforted by that thought!

(Note: My sister lives alone as a widow. She has reached the age of eighty-six years. She recently received a triple heart bypass.)

17

The Farm, 1970

We learned early on about the "empty nest." Our two older sons had begun the pursuit of their careers, one in medical school to be an OB-GYN, who graduated at the top of his class, and the second in medical technology in the United States Navy. (He made us proud as valedictorian of his class at the Great Lakes Naval Training Center in Chicago, Illinois.) The third son entered a prep school on the Gulf Coast. Remaining at home was the baby of the family, a fourteen-year-old boy with all the characteristics of a cowboy.

We found for him a quarter horse, a "Paint," also fourteen years old, and a farm to go with it. The well-trained horse with ample experience proved to be his teacher and the two won numerous trophies in the local and surrounding counties in quarter horse competition.

As the interest and activities on the farm grew, we found ourselves prepared to move on to another horizon—wide-open country on our 350-acre spread. My only fear was losing the amenities of the city: its water and sewage. Our daily delivery of the Memphis *Commercial Appeal* would be missed, as well as the weekly service of trash removal. Little did I realize that well water was much purer than tap water, and septic tanks had been improved. There was nothing to worry about. When I called the county extension office to inquire about trash pick-up, I was told to find a gulley! Fortunately, before long, as the city folks moved out, a regular pick-up service began.

We built a rustic house to go with its surroundings in the nearby woods and creek. Soon our quarter horse was joined by a stallion and seventeen mares. Along with the equines, we began experimenting with cattle and decided upon a herd of a new French breed, the Charolais.

I knew nothing about this new venture. I read a lot of Thoreau and bought a book on rural sociology. My husband soon taught me to ride—I even learned how to blow dry a steer in preparation for the county fair!

It was the mid-seventies. The war in Vietnam came to an embarrassing close. President Richard Nixon had been impeached and later pardoned. Marijuana entered the lives of so many school and college children. Its use, coupled with the hallucinogenic drugs, added to the alcohol abuse already underway. We were happy to be in the country and part of the county family. But other fears entered my life as a rural housewife.

The copperhead den in the backwoods gulley soon let us knows that we had invaded their territory. I often found them stretched out in the afternoon sun on the side steps. "Watch where you step" was our motto. Later the cotton-mouthed moccasins appeared, and yes, when they open their mouths, you could easily see that they were white, hence the name "cottonmouth."

I learned that it's the short fat snakes to avoid. The long, slithery black snakes are harmless. Even they can be scary when you seen them leap out of a hole in the ground in your flowerbed.

Soon after we moved into our new home, the radio and TV carried news of a black bear crossing the Mississippi River at Memphis, about 120 miles south. The Tennessee Wildlife Resources Agency was sure that it was seeking companions at the other end of the state in the Smoky Mountains. For several days, I expressed my concern. I knew that our farm was a perfect habitat for bears—a running creek, blackberries, acorns—but my husband scoffed at the thought.

The huge cypress, walnut, and pecan trees surrounding the house created a daily ritual of raking. The wheelbarrow was always full and ready to be emptied.

When leaving the house one evening, we noticed that the leaves and brush had been scooped out as if in search of something. We attributed it to the many raccoons.

The next morning, I continued with the yard work while our three dogs lay by. When I went into the house for a break, I heard our dogs barking ferociously at a black bear that had appeared out of nowhere. They quickly chased it down the hill to the creek as I frantically tried to reach the wildlife officers by phone. I was told that I could not go out and shoot it—it was considered an endangered species. At this time, I was in such an emotional state, that I shook when told that nothing would prevent it from coming after me if I frightened it.

The bear proceeded to Alabama by way of the creek. It was shot there by residents who were fishing close by.

When my husband suggested spending six months of the year in Pensacola, Florida, at a lovely condominium on the beach, with our retired navy friends, I jumped at the chance.

18

The Condominium, 1980

Our decision to have a respite in Florida was the result of a lot of thinking through and preparation. We were financially sound; our sons had married and presented us with eleven grandchildren in a ten-year period. But leaving "home" for us was a big step in an unknown territory.

Our youngest son was delighted to assume the responsibility of the horses. We realized that the herd of cattle would be burdensome. We reluctantly got out of that business and were relieved.

My husband's position in the symphony orchestra was not easy to fill, so he took a leave of absence while we were away. His music was his love before and even after me! Our two youngest sons took over management of our two local music and technology businesses, and I retired from directing the tutorial program for children with learning disabilities. I remained on the advisory board of the Tennessee Branch of the International Dyslexia Association and continue to serve as an advocate.

The condominium we bought on the Gulf Shore was only five miles from the Pensacola Naval Air Station. Twelve other military retirees bought into it simultaneously. Although most were navy, the group included several USAF officers who were compatible. We were all seniors, and, if I might say, the husbands were truly of "the greatest generation." The bond with this group was instantaneous. The participation in World War II was never a subject of conversation and the degree of rank was never discussed. They had done their jobs well and were grateful they were among the survivors.

My dear husband told me before we arrived to please not talk about our health or our grandchildren! Sadly, for him, everyone there talked about *their* health and *their* grandchildren. We partied and played golf.

A young black man served as our custodian. Filipino girls cleaned the units weekly.

The only weakness in our camaraderie was the dislike of a retired Jewish officer who had served under Bobby Kennedy in the attorney general's office. He and his lovely wife were outstanding in their graciousness to all of us. They were disliked by some only because they were Jews, proving that bigotry exists in good times as well as bad.

We had no hurricanes to reach our area in the fifteen years we were there. The January and February days were cold and misty. At times, we could not see the gulf waters for the fog.

President Lyndon Johnson suffered through the conclusion of the Vietnam War and declared a war on poverty. Jimmy Carter failed in his single term in office.

We saw the presidential administration change hands from President Jimmy Carter to Ronald Reagan, who asked Russia to tear down the Berlin Wall—and they did! The world seemed settled, but a Muslim tyrant, Saddam Hussein, was stirring and preparing to invade Kuwait as President George Herbert Walker Bush took office.

President Bush was of our generation, a family man who had enlisted in WWII as a young pilot. Later, as a Texas businessman, he entered politics and served in a number of capacities before assuming the presidency: ambassador to China, head of the CIA, and vice president to Ronald Reagan. We felt comfortable with his decision to go to war against Iraq. That war was called Desert Storm, and it was just that. A war in the desert, hot and dry. Scud missiles were born and feared. It was a new kind of war for those of us at home. We were able to watch it in progress.

That was what we did. Suddenly, life on the beaches and golf courses seemed less appealing. We sat up late at night watching our courageous journalists as they risked their lives to bring us the war on our television screens in our condo.

Sadly, the war ended before we could bring down the culprit. President Bush simply did not want to continue. The loss of our young men tormented him. He ordered everyone home.

19

A Slow Progression into Our Good-bye

My husband's illness began long before our good times in Florida. The symptoms at first were not recognizable, only frustrating to me and to him.

He could not walk down the flight of stairs in our home without knocking off all of the pictures that hung on the inside wall. So clumsy! He could not walk on the grass. He was unsteady when walking side by side with me. On occasion, he would ask me to walk behind him for fear of knocking me down. Forget walking in the dark! That was totally impossible.

When playing bridge, I noticed he always scooped up the cards with his whole hand to brush them off the table. He could not pick up small objects with any dexterity. His penmanship was legible but shaky. Ironically, he was able to manage our business affairs as well as he always had. He was an overachiever.

Giving up playing his beloved trombone hurt him and me the most. He had a gifted ability in expressing himself through that instrument. His signing off as a member of the symphony orchestra saddened both of us. We consulted a number of neurologists in Tennessee. The diagnosis was idiopathic peripheral neuropathy. Further testing revealed atrophy, cerebellum degeneration. Ironically, he died from vancomycin resistant bacteria following a routine gall bladder operation.

It was a horrific death for him and all of us—his four sons, their wives, children, and me. Being extremely contagious, he was confined to an isolated room and we were required, for our protection, to wear caps, masks, robes, gloves, and shoe covers before entering his room. The culprits destroyed his blood platelets, resulting in thrombocytopenia purpura.

I truly believe his suffering was minimal, as he was deeply sedated and died peacefully.

An editorial in the local newspaper at the time of his death lauded his life's work in music and said, "God's trombones would have a new player." Six months following that, the community opened the Krider Performing Arts Center. He was one of the honorees.

He truly believed that, without music, any child was poor.

20

Widowhood

We had sold our home on the front side of the farm to a former Secret Service agent of President George H.W. Bush. We built another home on the backside of the farm two miles away. This overlooked a large pond and was surrounded by woods that sheltered deer, wild turkeys, even coyotes!

Finding myself a widow six weeks before our fiftieth wedding anniversary, in 1999, was a blow far greater than I ever anticipated. I cried incessantly for an entire day before I realized that in my selfishness I had ignored my sons and their families. They were hurting too.

The void after so many years of companionship was huge. Friends I never knew I had came forth to offer comfort and food. Notes and letters of condolence were endless. I got comfort by acknowledging each one. I soon developed camaraderie with my widowed friends.

I have now completed my seventh year of living alone. A gift of a Saint Bernard puppy from my second son converted my self-pity to self-reliance. I quickly found out that I was capable of sustaining an enjoyable life on the farm with this big, slobbering fuzzy. I named her "Sweet Georgia Brown."

Following her arrival, it was catch-up time for my own well-being. I had not had a physical since my total knee-joint replacement ten years previously. I made an appointment immediately.

My internist completed the examination by giving me the necessary packet for an occult blood test to check out any bleeding from the colon, and he then suggested that I have a colonoscopy in lieu of that, since I had never had one. I did not hesitate. I made an appointment with a local surgeon immediately.

Fortunately for me, a benign polyp was found and removed. Then another one, a malignant small mass, was discovered. Surgery at Vanderbilt University Medical Center in Nashville required removal of ten inches of my colon. There was no lymph node involvement. No therapy followed, but recovery at home took some time.

Two years later, during a routine mammography, a small lesion was noted. Ultrasound confirmed that a biopsy was necessary. A small, non-aggressive cancer was discovered. My oncologist called it "a little c." It was not the Big C. When asked if I wanted a lumpectomy or a total radical, I accepted the latter. Again, there was no lymph node involvement. No therapy was required. Taking tamoxifen, the common medication to prevent the recurrence, was not an option for me due to an estrogen-induced blood clot I had experienced following menopause. Blood tests for "markers" follows every four months. Recovery from this surgery took little time, nothing like the invasive colon surgery. I drove myself to the grocery four days later.

The words of the late Pope John Paul II, "Be not afraid," sustained me throughout. I was terrified. I am a much stronger person because of these experiences.

Mothers of children with learning problems in school continued to call me for help. As long as there are children they cannot teach, schools can relegate them to "alternative schools," claiming behavior problems and turning them into classroom casualties. Lack of funding at the state or federal level is no excuse for the lack of conscience in local school administrations. I realize that my overly developed conscience originated in the classrooms of the Catholic girls' school I was privileged to attend. It truly gave me the courage to speak out against injustices. Being needed by so many caring mothers fortified me and burst the bubble of loneliness I found myself engulfed in. Does a perfect marriage ever exist? We were from geographically different parts of the country, reared in entirely different home environments, and of different religions—although he was converted to the Catholic faith by a navy chaplain—but our common goals and values gave us the spiritual power to embrace a life together for as long as we both would live.

Through our many travels, we continued to grow. We marveled at the harmony found in the blending of color and cultures in Hawaii. This was so unlike the caste system that still exists in Mexico with mud huts to palaces, children diving in the Pacific for pennies and the wealthy on the mountains above reveling in their affluence. In England in 1995, we found beautiful girls "of color" speaking grammatically correct English with English accents as clerks in the famous Harrod's. Asian Indians, Orientals, Europeans, and Muslims shopped unaware of ethnic differences.

On a return trip from San Francisco, we found ourselves in that city's huge airport waiting for a call to board our flight home. My husband asked me if I realized that besides the airline employees we were probably the only Caucasians there.

This great country continues to be a melting pot, one founded on the absolutes of the founders of our Constitution. We are multicultural. Whites (Caucasians) are now in the minority, and reverse discrimination is apparent. Are we teaching children the value of building character with firm beliefs in honesty and wholesome behavior? As an advocate for the importance of teaching reading, I renege in teaching those who have not been taught right from wrong. Otherwise, we will produce a group of individuals who just might end up as community leaders, or Heaven forbid, in Washington with no clue about nobility, acceptable deportment, and integrity—truly without conscience.

Epilogue

When I began writing this journal it was to explore my growth through my life in the twentieth century. Whoever said, "The more things change, the more they remain the same" was right on target in defining life throughout that century continuing into this one.

World War II followed Depression-induced poverty. War of some kind, somewhere continued intermittently throughout the century, along with some decades of capitalistic success. Presently, we are engaged in a war in the Middle East oddly called "Iraqi Freedom" in hopes of democratizing the area. A third world war is in the green room awaiting the staging of nuclear arms by Iran and North Korea, both of whom want to increase their world stature by getting into the act.

Bigotry and discrimination are as much alive today as they were in my growing up years. As the Irish (Micks), the Polish (honkies), the Italians (wops), the Jews (kikes), the blacks (niggers) battled it out, our nation survived. But in most cities, you will find that they prefer to segregate themselves into their own communities. We have lived through the era of mass immigration from Europe and are now faced with the exodus of thousands of Mexicans, posing new challenges in illiteracy and poverty.

Black children lead in those areas. Bill Cosby, the well-known actor/comedian, has championed his race directly by pointing out the problem they bring to themselves—and he is being criticized for it!

Mexicans recently staged a national march protesting present immigration laws. Rather than polarize, we need to make a great effort to compromise. We have always told our sons that they came into this world no better than anyone else. To succeed, they must prove themselves. All of our forefathers came as immigrants at one time. Some arrived early and are under the illusion that they are better than others.

The century saw tremendous strides in the development of frightful weaponry. By way of NASA, the National Aeronautics and Space Administration, we actually landed a man on the moon (Neil Armstrong) and are continuing to probe scientific possibilities in outer space. Satellites are everywhere receiving and transmitting signals. Space stations record information daily. The tragedies in the death of astronauts flying missions that should have been aborted still haunt us. NASA's work continues.

Advancement in medicine have surpassed those in space exploration—we have discovered antibiotics to combat new bacterial diseases, immunizations for dreaded contagious illnesses, and the cause of HIV and its prevention. Our physicians were given tools they desperately needed. We have a long way to go to halt the spread of e-coli, malaria, smallpox and anthrax.

Some say that our environment is being threatened by global warming. My late mother, born in the nineteenth century, always said that the preponderance of cancer had to be related to automobile emissions. The transportation in her day was by horse and buggy. The emissions from that made great fertilizer!

We did not have oncology as a course in nursing/medical school in the early part of the twentieth century. The increase of carcinoma today is frightening. We can be comforted in knowing that research is being conducted throughout the world. Cancer centers are located in all of our metropolitan areas and beyond. As a cancer survivor, I can relate to the comments of the late journalist, Molly Ivins, a breast cancer victim, who said, "First they mutilate you, then they poison you, then you die!" We must campaign for improved therapy and, above all, for a cure!

The anomalies associated with homosexuality continue to plague us. We were and are confronted by condemning the sin and forgiving the sinners who have come "out of the closet." Their lifestyles have changed our society, even infringed upon the sanctity of marriage between man and a woman. How we treat them will play upon our consciences.

Women were given the opportunity to gain equality in all fields. In colleges in the forties and fifties, one seldom saw a girl admitted to medical or law school. Few were accepted in our service academies.

Today, Dr. Kay Jamison, as a professor in psychiatry at Johns Hopkins Medical School, is bi-polar and has written books on the subject. She succeeds in helping so many others because of her personal understanding of the problem.

Dr. Condoleezza Rice taught at Stanford University, is an expert on Russian studies, and has succeeded as the secretary of state for the United States.

Sandra Day O'Connor, who grew up on a ranch in Arizona, was appointed as a justice of the Supreme Court after graduating from Stanford Law School.

Everyone has seen Nancy Grace, a criminal lawyer, who has a nationally televised program to inform her listeners about the law and those who break it.

Oprah Winfrey rose from the slums in the poverty of black America by receiving an education and becoming known worldwide for her philanthropy, derived from her success as a television talk show hostess.

These are but a few.

The digital age is transforming our lives. The explosion of communication in the world of television and the Internet have changed and even interfered with everyday life. Families seldom gather around the table for meals; busy schedules away from home preclude the togetherness we once enjoyed.

The quest for the truth and the search for spirituality continues to challenge us. No one exemplified love and forbearance more than the late Pope John Paul II, a Pole whose papacy exceeded all expectations. His funeral was the largest ever held in the Vatican in Rome, with dignitaries from all over the world in attendance. These are large shoes to fill for Cardinal Ratzinger, who has succeeded him. Turning swords into plowshares will not be easy.

Those of good conscience must be aroused and deeply disturbed about what is going on around us here and abroad. It is time to help in advancing the new cultures within our communities through literacy and understanding.

The great novelist William James said that three things in human life are important. The first is to be kind. The second is to be kind. The third is to be kind. I hope my sons will remember that!

978-0-595-43634-7
0-595-43634-X

www.ingramcontent.com/pod-product-compliance
Lightning Source LLC
Chambersburg PA
CBHW030346290526
45785CB00004B/1621